learn to draw

Cats & Kittens

Learn to draw and color **26** different
kitties, step by easy step,
shape by simple shape!

Illustrated by Diana Fisher

Walter Foster

Getting Started

When you look closely at the drawings in this book, you'll notice that they're made up of basic shapes, such as circles, triangles, and rectangles. To draw all your favorite felines, just start with simple shapes as you see here. It's easy and fun!

Circles are used to draw a standing cat's chest and hips.

Ovals are good for starting out a seated feline.

Triangles are purr-fect for most cats' ears.

Coloring Tips

There's more than one way to bring your fave felines to life on paper—you can use crayons, markers, or colored pencils. Just be sure you have plenty of good natural colors, such as black, brown, orange, pink, and green.

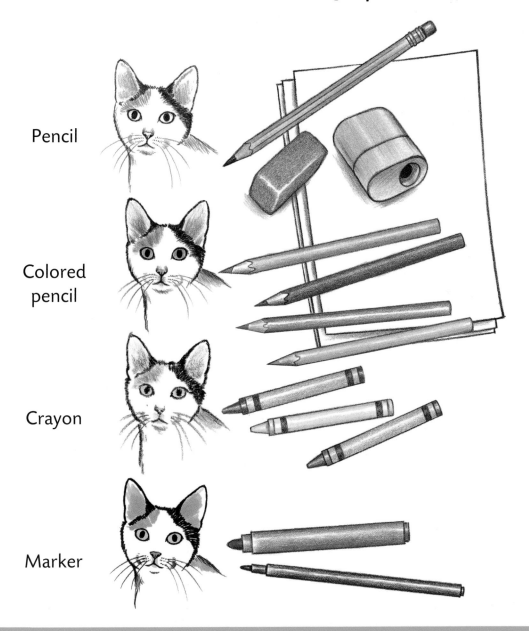

Pencil

Colored pencil

Crayon

Marker

Persian Cat

The popular Persian is known for its long, luxurious coat. But its face, neck, body, and legs are all short—so is its bushy tail!

5

fun fact

The Cat Fanciers' Association (CFA) categorizes Persians by fur color and pattern, including solid color, silver and golden, shaded and smoke, tabby, particolor, bicolor, and Himalayan classes. But all these Persian types have one important thing in common: They require a lot of grooming! Persians have longer, thicker coats than any other domestic cats—their topcoat can be up to 5 inches long!

6

Egyptian Mau

The Mau cat sports both spots and stripes!
And this social kitty has a reputation for being
playful as well as graceful.

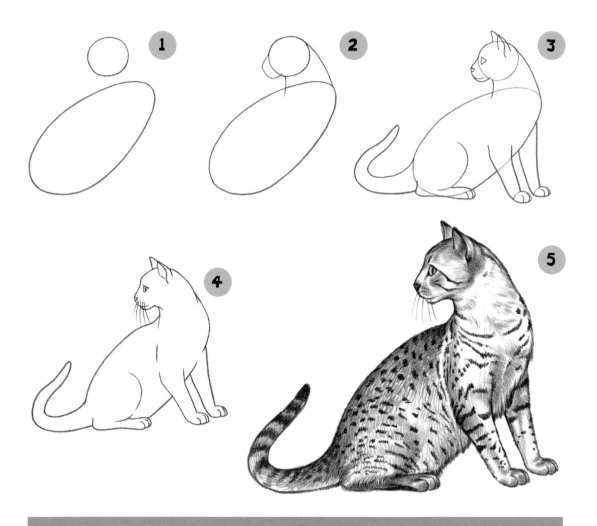

British Shorthair

The best words to describe this feline are large and round! And circles and ovals are the purr-fect shapes for drawing this quiet cat!

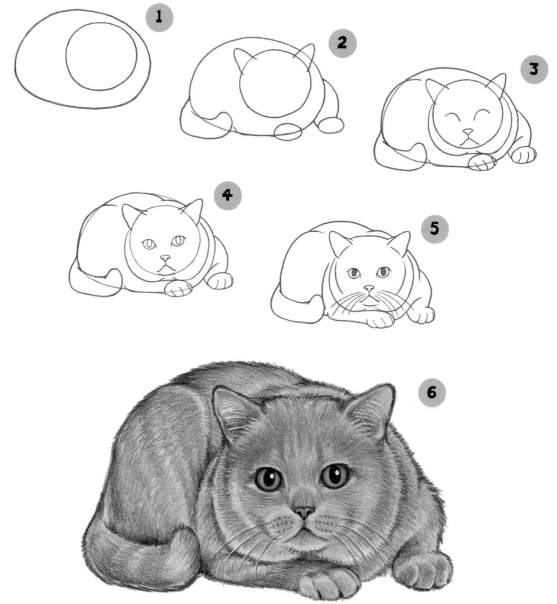

Selkirk Rex Kitten

Selkirk Rex kittens often have shaggy, rumpled-looking fur. When they reach adulthood, their wavy locks become curly coats.

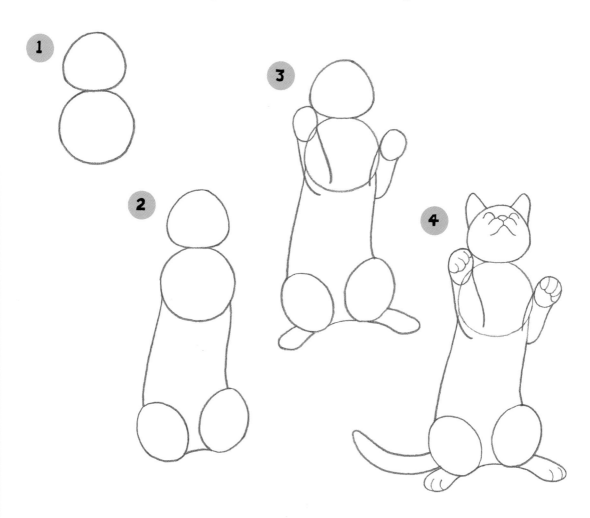

fun fact

The Selkirk Rex is a natural breed that was discovered in the United States in 1987. Like the Cornish Rex and the Devon Rex, this breed has a curly coat. But with its stronger, rounder body, it looks very different from its fellow "Rex" cats!

5

6

7

Abyssinian Kitten

Abys are short-haired cats with strong bodies—and stronger personalities! These curious kitties are intelligent and outgoing.

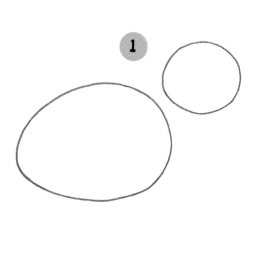

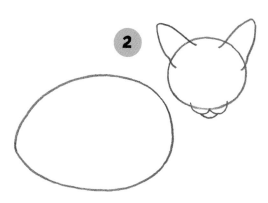

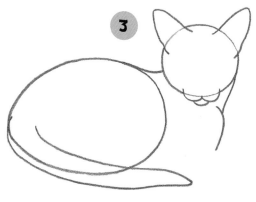

The first documented Aby came from Ethiopia in 1868—but many believe that this elegant breed is a descendant of the cats of ancient Egypt! The mummified cats found in Pharaohs' tombs are similar to today's Abyssinian in many ways.

Ocicat

Despite its large, muscular body, the spotted Ocicat is graceful. This exotic-looking tabby has a long tail that tapers to a point.

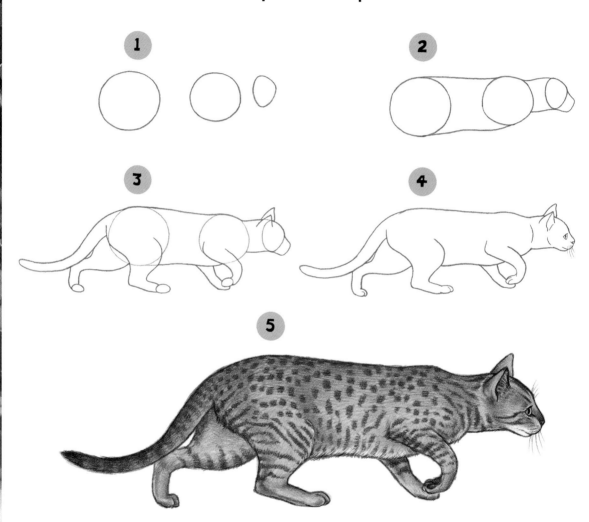

Persian Himalayan Kitten

This snuggly ball of fur is a special kind of Persian. It has a "color point" pattern, with darker shading on its tail, legs, ears, and face.

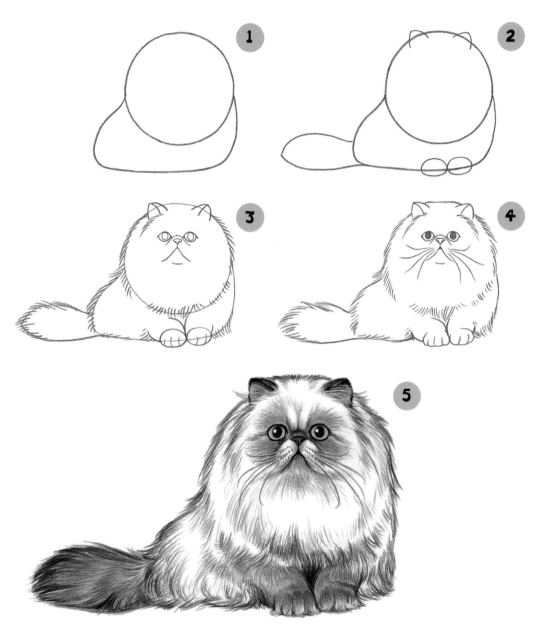

Cornish Rex

With a wavy coat, a wiry body, a whiplike tail, and prominent "bat" ears, the cornish Rex is easy to notice and hard to forget!

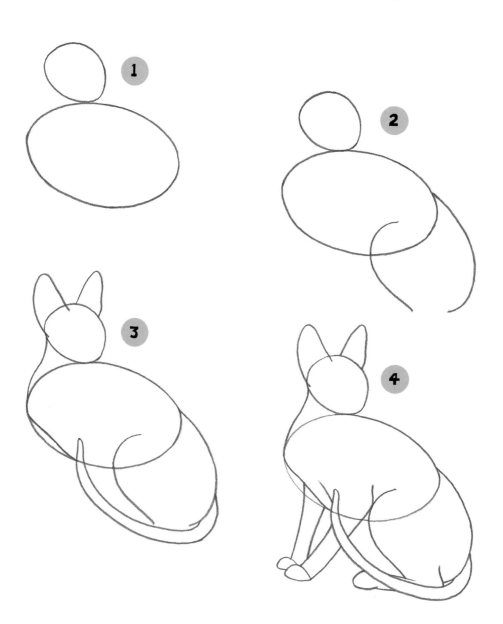

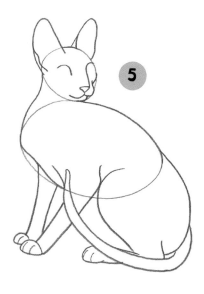

5

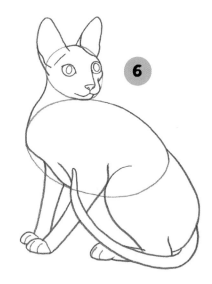

6

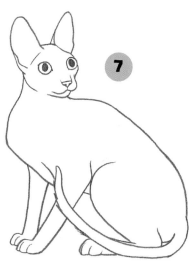

7

8

fun fact

It may look like something from outer space, but the Cornish Rex is actually named after a bunny! The owner of the first Cornish Rex named the breed for its plush coat, which feels similar to the velveteen coat of the Rex breed of rabbits.

Maine Coon

It's easy to see where the gentle giant of the cat world got its name! This Maine native has a bushy, ringed tail—like a raccoon's!

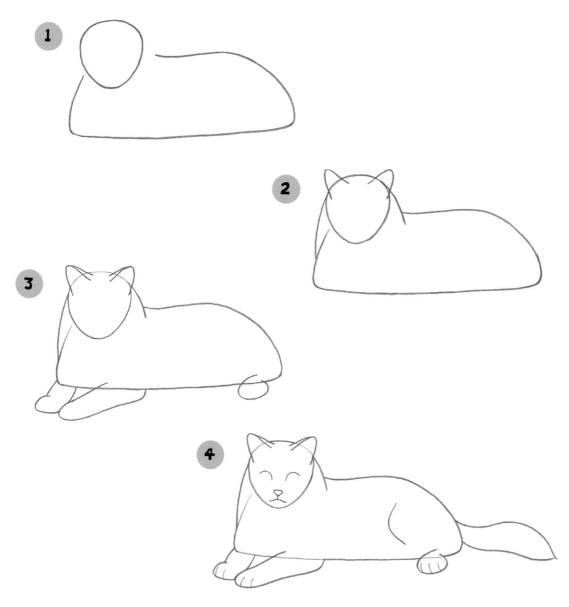

fun fact

The Maine Coon is the oldest American breed and the first native American show cat! Although it now places second in breed popularity, the Coon comes first in size. Some males weigh 20 pounds or more, and this Yankee cat is four times the size of the Singapura, the smallest cat breed.

Ragdoll

This soft, fluffy cat is so relaxed that it flops like a rag doll when picked up! An affectionate breed, Ragdolls love to cuddle.

Manx

The Manx is a mouser with only a small bump for a tail! And with its longer rear legs, this kitty shows off its "rumpy riser."

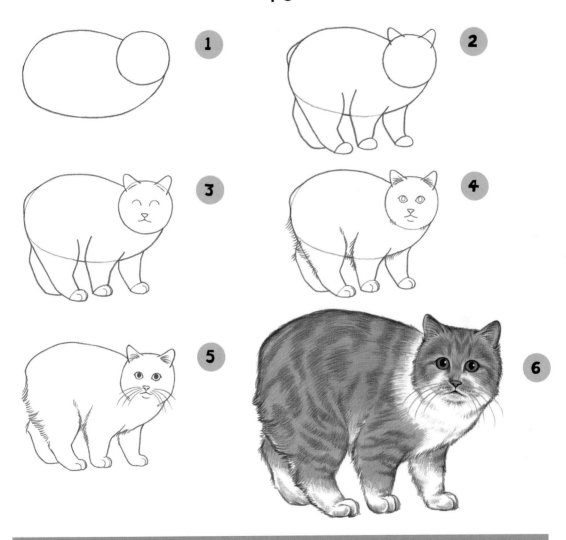

fun fact   The Manx breed comes from the Isle of Man, off the coast of Britain. There tailless cats are so common that when a native farmer learned that rumors about cats having tails were true, he said, "That must look really funny, all those cats with tails."

Curious Kittens

Cats have a reputation for being curious—but kittens take curiosity to the extreme! These young felines are eager to explore everything the world has to offer!

Turkish Angora

This beautiful breed has a slender body, a long neck, a wedge-shaped head, and sometimes two eyes that are different colors. The Turkish Angora is playful and devoted!

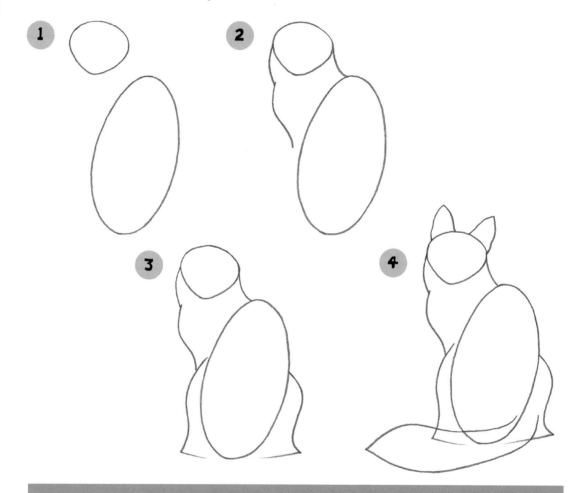

fun fact

The Turkish Angora is one of the national treasures of its homeland, Turkey. It was the first long-haired cat to be brought to Europe and was the darling of European aristocracy in the 1700s. But the breed lost popularity, and these cats would be extinct today if not for the Turkish zoos that saved them!

Russian Blue

Quiet-loving Blues can happily sit still for hours. To draw this cat in its comfy pose, begin with marshmallow shapes for its head and body.

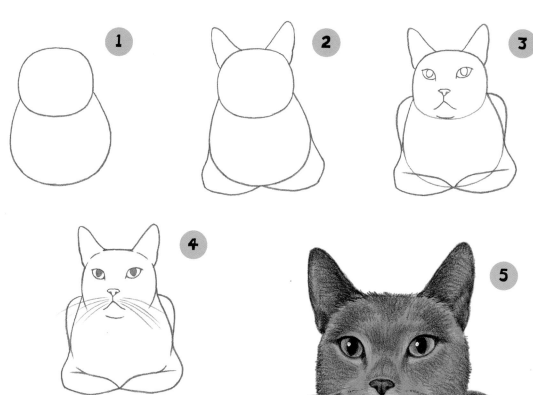

fun fact

As you might guess from its name, the Russian Blue comes from Russia, where it was discovered by the British about 200 years ago. This breed has had many names in the past, including "Russian Shorthair," "Maltese Blue," "Archangel Blue," and "Foreign Blue."

American Curl

The curl is the only breed with ears that curl backward. It's a good thing this friendly feline loves to be center of attention!

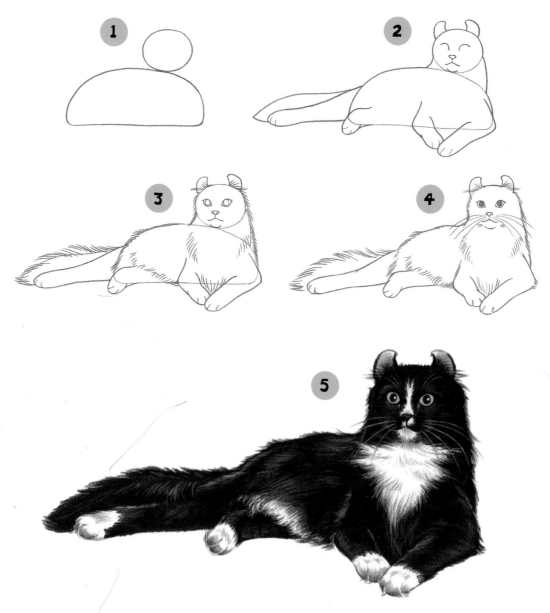

Norwegian Forest Cats

The Wegie is a furry feline with a thick, heavy coat of fur. Its mane and tail are fluffy, and its triangular ears are straight and tall!

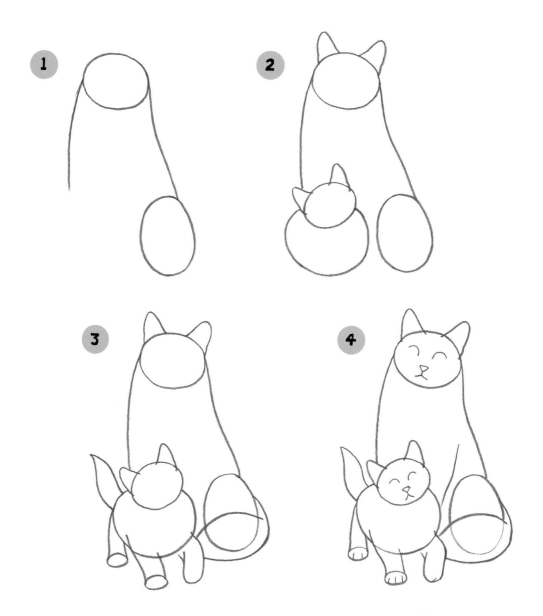

5

fun fact

Vikings (Scandinavian seafarers) liked to have cats on their ships to fight pest populations, so they picked up mousers at ports around the world; they brought the first cats to Norway around the year 1000. Cold Nordic winters favored cats with sturdy builds and thick coats, so these imported cats eventually developed into a new breed: Norwegian Forest Cats.

6

7

Scottish Fold

With unusual flat, folded ears, a round head, and golden eyes, the Scottish Fold looks like the feline version of an owl!

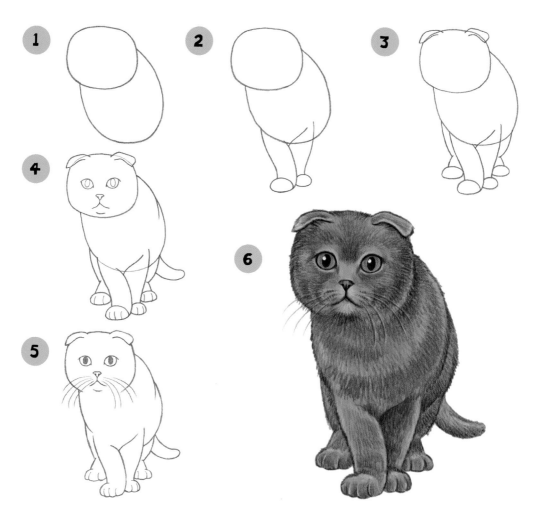

fun fact

Scottish Folds aren't bred with other Folds because their kittens can have crippling skeletal problems. To keep this breed healthy, Folds are mated with Scottish Straights (cats from the same bloodline without folded ears) and American or British Shorthairs.

Birman Kitten

The round white paws on this breed—also known as "The Sacred cat of Burma"—distinguish it from other color-point varieties.

Traditional Siamese

This "old-fashioned" cat looks different than the triangular-headed Siamese, but both breed types are talkative and attention-loving.

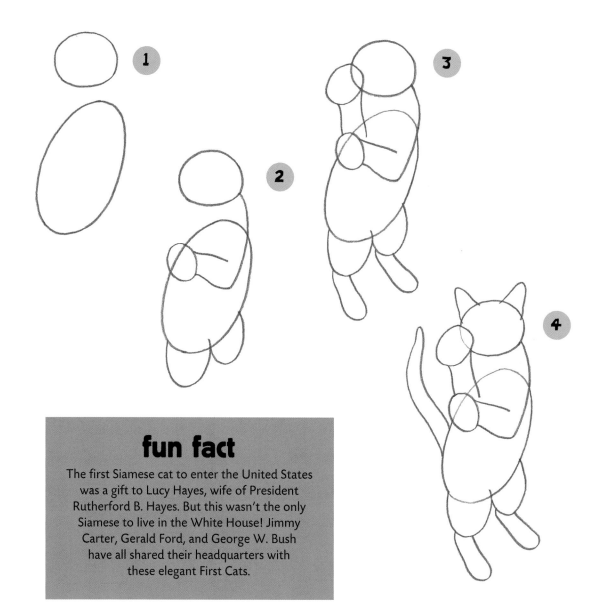

fun fact

The first Siamese cat to enter the United States was a gift to Lucy Hayes, wife of President Rutherford B. Hayes. But this wasn't the only Siamese to live in the White House! Jimmy Carter, Gerald Ford, and George W. Bush have all shared their headquarters with these elegant First Cats.

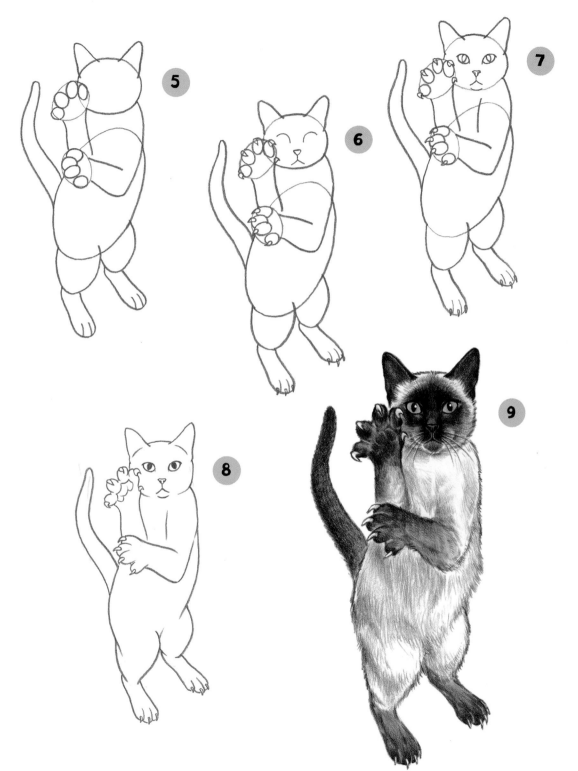

Japanese Bobtail

Most members of this centuries-old bobtail breed display a patched calico pattern called "mi-ke," which the Japanese consider lucky.

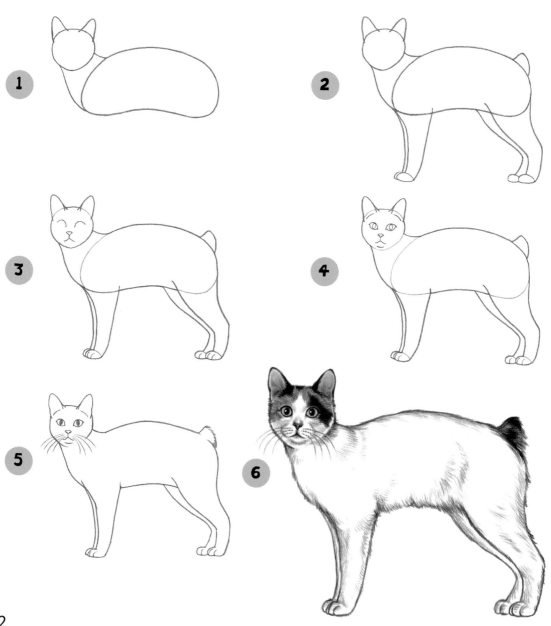

Sphynx

The huge, triangular ears of this hairless cat are hard to miss! And its wrinkled skin, wide-set eyes, and large paws also draw attention.

fun fact

The Sphynx is the only modern hairless cat breed—but it isn't the first of its kind. The ancient Aztecs also kept hairless cats; unfortunately, the Aztec breed is now extinct.

Somali

The wild-looking Somali is a long-haired version of the Abyssinian. This feline's coat is thickest at the ruff, haunches, and tail.

fun fact

The Somali's body shape, reddish-brown fur color, and full coat combine to make this cat look like another animal altogether. So it should come as no surprise that the Somali's nickname is "fox cat."

Persian Kitten

This adorable, pudgy-bodied, sweet-faced kitten is just one example of why Persians are the most popular cat in the world!

Devon Rex Kitten

You'd never guess by its size, but this thin-bodied breed loves to eat! This small kitty needs lots of food to fuel its active lifestyle.

fun fact

The Cornish Rex and Devon Rex look similar—and, because they both have "Rex" in their name, people think they're related. But these cats come from two different bloodlines—if you mate the two, the kittens will have straight hair!

American Wirehair Kitten

A coarse coat is the most outstanding feature of this feline! Its short curls give this cat's fur a rough, wiry appearance.

Exotic

The Exotic is a short-haired version of the Persian. Like its long-haired relatives, this cat hides a sweet nature behind a grumpy look!

fun fact

When you mate two Exotics, what do you get? Exotic kittens . . . and Persian kittens too! Exotics produce both short-haired and long-haired kittens—and it's nearly impossible to tell the two breeds apart until the cats are about 8 weeks old!

Korat

In Thailand, this shiny-coated cat is considered a symbol of good luck! The breed is also known for being vocal and affectionate.